START HERE

Hello and welcome to the digital marketing planner. If this is your first interaction with me, then hello!

My name is Brandon Breshears. I'm the host of the Veterinary Marketing Podcast and the Owner of Maverick Digital Marketing, my digital marketing agency.

I've built this digital planner as a way to put all of your content and campaigns in one place to help give you clarity about your digital marketing.

I've also built out free trainings around this planner to help you get more out of it. Go to:
www.veterinarymarketingpodcast.com/planner to get your free trainings now.

If you ever feel uncertain of what you should do with your company's digital marketing, then this planner is the perfect place to start.

SOCIAL MEDIA FOLLOWERS

Channel	Jan	Feb	Mar	Apr	May	June	July	Aug	Sept	Oct	Nov	Dec
Facebook												
Twitter												
Instagram												
Pinterest												
Youtube												
Email												

This Years Stats		Last Years Stats	
Facebook		Facebook	
Twitter		Twitter	
Instagram		Instagram	
Pinterest		Pinterest	
Youtube		Youtube	
Email		Email	

NOTES

NOTES

GOALS

HOW OFTEN DO YOU WANT TO EMAIL YOUR LIST _____

_____

HOW OFTEN DO YOU WANT TO PROMOTE SPECIAL OFFERS _____

_____

HOW MANY NEW CLIENTS PER MONTH DO YOU WANT _____

_____

HOW MANY MONTHLY EMAILS DO YOU WANT TO GATHER _____

_____

HOW MANY SOCIAL POSTS PER WEEK _____

_____

HOW MANY NEW BLOG POSTS DO YOU WANT _____

_____

HOW MANY SOCIAL FOLLOWERS DO YOU WANT

f _____ FOLLOWERS BY _____ / _____ / _____

⊙ _____ FOLLOWERS BY _____ / _____ / _____

▶ _____ FOLLOWERS BY _____ / _____ / _____

🐦 _____ FOLLOWERS BY _____ / _____ / _____

HOW MANY FUNNELS DO YOU WANT TO BUILD _____

_____

WHAT KEY SERVICES DO YOU WANT TO PROMOTE _____

_____

WHAT AD PLATFORMS DO YOU WANT TO USE & LEARN ON _____

_____

DIGITAL MARKETING ASSETS

KEYWORDS/HASHTAG TRACKER

Subject:

- _____
- _____
- _____
- _____
- _____
- _____
- _____
- _____

Subject:

- _____
- _____
- _____
- _____
- _____
- _____
- _____
- _____

Subject:

- _____
- _____
- _____
- _____
- _____
- _____
- _____
- _____

Subject:

- _____
- _____
- _____
- _____
- _____
- _____
- _____
- _____

Subject:

- _____
- _____
- _____
- _____
- _____
- _____
- _____
- _____

Subject:

- _____
- _____
- _____
- _____
- _____
- _____
- _____
- _____

KEYWORDS/HASHTAG TRACKER

Subject:

- _____
- _____
- _____
- _____
- _____
- _____
- _____
- _____

Subject:

- _____
- _____
- _____
- _____
- _____
- _____
- _____
- _____

Subject:

- _____
- _____
- _____
- _____
- _____
- _____
- _____
- _____

Subject:

- _____
- _____
- _____
- _____
- _____
- _____
- _____
- _____

Subject:

- _____
- _____
- _____
- _____
- _____
- _____
- _____
- _____

Subject:

- _____
- _____
- _____
- _____
- _____
- _____
- _____
- _____

HEADLINE FORMULAS

BEFORE-AFTER-BRIDGE

- Custom Audience
- Describe a world where the problem is solved
- Explain how you go there

PROBLEM-AGITATE-SOLVE

- Find the problem
- Agitate the problem
- Solve the probelm

FEATURES-ADVANTAGES-BENEFITS

- What you can do for the reader
- Why that is helpful
- What that means for the reader

CLEAR-CONCISE-COMPELLING-CREDIBLE

- Keep the headline clear
- Keep it concise
- Have a compelling angle
- Write with credibility

USEFUL-URGENT-UNIQUE-ULTRA-SPECIFIC

- Be useful to the reader
- Create a sense of urgency
- Convey the idea that the benefits are unique
- Be ultra specific

HEADLINE FORMULAS

ATTENTION-INTEREST-DESIRE-ACTION

- Grab the readers attention
- Give readers fresh information
- Outline the benefits of your services and give proof
- Ask for a response

ALLITERATION-FACTS-OPINIONS-REPETITION-EXAMPLES-STATISTICS-THREES

- Post with alliteration or facts or threes

THE 5 BASIC OBJECTIONS

- Not enough money
- Not enough time
- It won't work for me
- I don't believe you
- I don't need it

PICTURE-PROMISE-PROVE-PUSH

- Paint a picture to grab attention
- Describe how you will deliver
- Provide support for your promise
- Ask reader to commit

PICTURE-PROMISE-PROVE-PUSH

- Create a cliffhanger

NOTES

NOTES

IDEAL CLIENT AVATAR WORKSHEET

NAME _____

AGE _____

GENDER _____

MARITAL STATUS _____

#/AGE OF CHILDREN _____

LOCATION _____

NUMBER OF PETS _____

TYPES OF PETS/ANIMALS _____

ANNUAL INCOME _____

LEVEL OF EDUCATION _____

OTHER _____

GOALS AND VALUES

GOALS:

VALUES:

SOURCES OF INFORMATION

BOOKS:

MAGAZINES:

BLOGS/WEBSITES:

CONFERENCES:

GURUS:

OTHER:

IDEAL CLIENT AVATAR WORKSHEET

CHALLENGES AND PAIN POINTS

CHALLENGES:

PAIN POINTS:

OBJECTIONS & ROLE IN PURCHASE PROCESS

OBJECTIONS:

ROLE IN THE PURCHASE PROCESS:

IDEAL CLIENT AVATAR WORKSHEET

NAME _____

AGE _____

GENDER _____

MARITAL STATUS _____

#/AGE OF CHILDREN _____

LOCATION _____

NUMBER OF PETS _____

TYPES OF PETS/ANIMALS _____

ANNUAL INCOME _____

LEVEL OF EDUCATION _____

OTHER _____

GOALS AND VALUES

GOALS:

VALUES:

SOURCES OF INFORMATION

BOOKS:

MAGAZINES:

BLOGS/WEBSITES:

CONFERENCES:

GURUS:

OTHER:

IDEAL CLIENT AVATAR WORKSHEET

CHALLENGES AND PAIN POINTS

CHALLENGES:

PAIN POINTS:

OBJECTIONS & ROLE IN PURCHASE PROCESS

OBJECTIONS:

ROLE IN THE PURCHASE PROCESS:

IDEAL CLIENT AVATAR WORKSHEET

NAME _____

AGE _____

GENDER _____

MARITAL STATUS _____

#/AGE OF CHILDREN _____

LOCATION _____

NUMBER OF PETS _____

TYPES OF PETS/ANIMALS _____

ANNUAL INCOME _____

LEVEL OF EDUCATION _____

OTHER _____

GOALS AND VALUES

GOALS:

VALUES:

SOURCES OF INFORMATION

BOOKS:

MAGAZINES:

BLOGS/WEBSITES:

CONFERENCES:

GURUS:

OTHER:

IDEAL CLIENT AVATAR WORKSHEET

CHALLENGES AND PAIN POINTS

CHALLENGES:

PAIN POINTS:

OBJECTIONS & ROLE IN PURCHASE PROCESS

OBJECTIONS:

ROLE IN THE PURCHASE PROCESS:

IDEAL CLIENT AVATAR WORKSHEET

NAME _____

AGE _____

GENDER _____

MARITAL STATUS _____

#/AGE OF CHILDREN _____

LOCATION _____

NUMBER OF PETS _____

TYPES OF PETS/ANIMALS _____

ANNUAL INCOME _____

LEVEL OF EDUCATION _____

OTHER _____

GOALS AND VALUES

GOALS:

VALUES:

SOURCES OF INFORMATION

BOOKS:

MAGAZINES:

BLOGS/WEBSITES:

CONFERENCES:

GURUS:

OTHER:

IDEAL CLIENT AVATAR WORKSHEET

CHALLENGES AND PAIN POINTS

CHALLENGES:

PAIN POINTS:

OBJECTIONS & ROLE IN PURCHASE PROCESS

OBJECTIONS:

ROLE IN THE PURCHASE PROCESS:

LANDING PAGE CHECKLIST

- [ ] MARKET CALLOUT
- [ ] CLEAR AND CONCISE
- [ ] EASILY UNDERSTOOD
- [ ] COMPELLING HEADLINE
- [ ] CTA ABOVE THE FOLD
- [ ] CONTRASTING BUTTON COLOR
- [ ] CUSTOM BUTTON TEXT
- [ ] SOCIAL PROOF
- [ ] VISIBLE PRIVACY POLICY AND TOS

- [ ] LIMITED NAVIGATION
- [ ] USE VISUAL CUES
- [ ] HERO SHOT
- [ ] LIMITED FORM FIELDS
- [ ] SOURCE CONGRUENCY
- [ ] BRAND CONSISTENCY
- [ ] ENABLE SHARING

LANDING PAGE OUTLINE

_____

_____

_____

_____

_____

_____

_____

_____

_____

_____

_____

_____

_____

_____

_____

_____

LANDING PAGE CHECKLIST

- [ ] MARKET CALLOUT
- [ ] CLEAR AND CONCISE
- [ ] EASILY UNDERSTOOD
- [ ] COMPELLING HEADLINE
- [ ] CTA ABOVE THE FOLD
- [ ] CONTRASTING BUTTON COLOR
- [ ] CUSTOM BUTTON TEXT
- [ ] SOCIAL PROOF
- [ ] VISIBLE PRIVACY POLICY AND TOS

- [ ] LIMITED NAVIGATION
- [ ] USE VISUAL CUES
- [ ] HERO SHOT
- [ ] LIMITED FORM FIELDS
- [ ] SOURCE CONGRUENCY
- [ ] BRAND CONSISTENCY
- [ ] ENABLE SHARING

LANDING PAGE OUTLINE

LANDING PAGE CHECKLIST

- [ ] MARKET CALLOUT
- [ ] CLEAR AND CONCISE
- [ ] EASILY UNDERSTOOD
- [ ] COMPELLING HEADLINE
- [ ] CTA ABOVE THE FOLD
- [ ] CONTRASTING BUTTON COLOR
- [ ] CUSTOM BUTTON TEXT
- [ ] SOCIAL PROOF
- [ ] VISIBLE PRIVACY POLICY AND TOS

- [ ] LIMITED NAVIGATION
- [ ] USE VISUAL CUES
- [ ] HERO SHOT
- [ ] LIMITED FORM FIELDS
- [ ] SOURCE CONGRUENCY
- [ ] BRAND CONSISTENCY
- [ ] ENABLE SHARING

LANDING PAGE OUTLINE

_____

_____

_____

_____

_____

_____

_____

_____

_____

_____

_____

_____

_____

_____

_____

_____

_____

LANDING PAGE CHECKLIST

- [ ] MARKET CALLOUT
- [ ] CLEAR AND CONCISE
- [ ] EASILY UNDERSTOOD
- [ ] COMPELLING HEADLINE
- [ ] CTA ABOVE THE FOLD
- [ ] CONTRASTING BUTTON COLOR
- [ ] CUSTOM BUTTON TEXT
- [ ] SOCIAL PROOF
- [ ] VISIBLE PRIVACY POLICY AND TOS

- [ ] LIMITED NAVIGATION
- [ ] USE VISUAL CUES
- [ ] HERO SHOT
- [ ] LIMITED FORM FIELDS
- [ ] SOURCE CONGRUENCY
- [ ] BRAND CONSISTENCY
- [ ] ENABLE SHARING

LANDING PAGE OUTLINE

_____

_____

_____

_____

_____

_____

_____

_____

_____

_____

_____

_____

_____

_____

_____

MONTH OF _____

Monday	Tuesday	Wednesday	Thursday	Friday	Saturday	Sunday

Awareness Goals:
_____
_____
_____
_____

Evaluation Goals:
_____
_____
_____
_____

Conversion & Retention Goals:
_____
_____
_____
_____

WEEK OF _____

Monday	Tuesday	Wednesday	Thursday	Friday	Saturday	Sunday

Awareness Goals:

Evaluation Goals:

Conversion & Retention Goals:

WEEK OF _____

Monday	Tuesday	Wednesday	Thursday	Friday	Saturday	Sunday

Awareness Goals:

_____
_____
_____
_____

Evaluation Goals:

_____
_____
_____
_____

Conversion & Retention Goals:

_____
_____
_____
_____

WEEK OF _____

Monday	Tuesday	Wednesday	Thursday	Friday	Saturday	Sunday

Awareness Goals:

_____
_____
_____

Evaluation Goals:

_____
_____
_____

Conversion & Retention Goals:

_____
_____
_____

WEEK OF

Monday	Tuesday	Wednesday	Thursday	Friday	Saturday	Sunday

Awareness Goals:

Evaluation Goals:

Conversion & Retention Goals:

WEEK OF ____

Monday	Tuesday	Wednesday	Thursday	Friday	Saturday	Sunday

Awareness Goals:

Evaluation Goals:

Conversion & Retention Goals:

DETAILED AD CAMPAIGN TRACKER

AD HEADLINE 1 _____

_____

AD HEADLINE 2 _____

_____

AD TEXT _____

_____

_____

_____

IMAGE IDEA _____

_____

URL _____

CALL TO ACTION

- ☐ SHOP NOW   ☐ DOWNLOAD   ☐ WATCH MORE   ☐ BOOK NOW
- ☐ LISTEN NOW   ☐ LEARN MORE   ☐ APPLY NOW   ☐ SIGN UP
- ☐ INSTALL NOW   ☐ DONATE NOW   ☐ USE APP   ☐ CONTACT US

AD TARGETS   AGE _____   LOCATION _____   GENDER _____

CUSTOM AUDIENCE _____   INTEREST _____

_____   _____

WHAT IS THE GOAL FOR THE AD?   ☐ AWARENESS ☐ EVALUATION ☐ CONVERSION

HOW WILL YOU TRACK SUCCESS? _____

_____

IS THE CALL TO ACTION CLEAR? ☐ YES ☐ NO   IS YOUR PIXEL INSTALLED? ☐ YES ☐ NO

AD BUDGET _____

AD DURATION _____ - _____

DETAILED AD CAMPAIGN TRACKER

AD HEADLINE 1 _____

_____

AD HEADLINE 2 _____

_____

AD TEXT _____

_____

_____

_____

IMAGE IDEA _____

_____

URL _____

CALL TO ACTION
☐ SHOP NOW   ☐ DOWNLOAD   ☐ WATCH MORE   ☐ BOOK NOW
☐ LISTEN NOW   ☐ LEARN MORE   ☐ APPLY NOW   ☐ SIGN UP
☐ INSTALL NOW   ☐ DONATE NOW   ☐ USE APP   ☐ CONTACT US

AD TARGETS AGE _____ LOCATION _____ GENDER _____

CUSTOM AUDIENCE _____ INTEREST _____

_____ _____

WHAT IS THE GOAL FOR THE AD? ☐ AWARENESS ☐ EVALUATION ☐ CONVERSION

HOW WILL YOU TRACK SUCCESS? _____

_____

IS THE CALL TO ACTION CLEAR? ☐ YES ☐ NO   IS YOUR PIXEL INSTALLED? ☐ YES ☐ NO

AD BUDGET _____

AD DURATION _____ - _____

DETAILED AD CAMPAIGN TRACKER

AD HEADLINE 1

_____

_____

AD HEADLINE 2

_____

_____

AD TEXT

_____

_____

_____

_____

IMAGE IDEA

_____

_____

URL

CALL TO ACTION
☐ SHOP NOW   ☐ DOWNLOAD   ☐ WATCH MORE   ☐ BOOK NOW

☐ LISTEN NOW   ☐ LEARN MORE   ☐ APPLY NOW   ☐ SIGN UP

☐ INSTALL NOW   ☐ DONATE NOW   ☐ USE APP   ☐ CONTACT US

AD TARGETS   AGE _____   LOCATION _____   GENDER _____

CUSTOM AUDIENCE _____   INTEREST _____

_____   _____

WHAT IS THE GOAL FOR THE AD?   ☐ AWARENESS   ☐ EVALUATION   ☐ CONVERSION

HOW WILL YOU TRACK SUCCESS? _____

_____

IS THE CALL TO ACTION CLEAR? ☐ YES ☐ NO   IS YOUR PIXEL INSTALLED? ☐ YES ☐ NO

AD BUDGET _____

AD DURATION _____ - _____

DETAILED AD CAMPAIGN TRACKER

AD HEADLINE 1 _____

_____

AD HEADLINE 2 _____

_____

AD TEXT _____

_____

_____

_____

IMAGE IDEA _____

_____

URL _____

CALL TO ACTION
☐ SHOP NOW ☐ DOWNLOAD ☐ WATCH MORE ☐ BOOK NOW
☐ LISTEN NOW ☐ LEARN MORE ☐ APPLY NOW ☐ SIGN UP
☐ INSTALL NOW ☐ DONATE NOW ☐ USE APP ☐ CONTACT US

AD TARGETS AGE _____ LOCATION _____ GENDER _____

CUSTOM AUDIENCE _____ INTEREST _____

_____ _____

WHAT IS THE GOAL FOR THE AD? ☐ AWARENESS ☐ EVALUATION ☐ CONVERSION

HOW WILL YOU TRACK SUCCESS? _____

_____

IS THE CALL TO ACTION CLEAR? ☐ YES ☐ NO   IS YOUR PIXEL INSTALLED? ☐ YES ☐ NO

AD BUDGET _____

AD DURATION _____ - _____

ADVERTISING TRACKER

DESCRIPTION

FORMAT

START DATE

END DATE

CLICKS

SALES

NOTES

DESCRIPTION

FORMAT

START DATE

END DATE

CLICKS

SALES

NOTES

ADVERTISING TRACKER

DESCRIPTION

FORMAT

START DATE

END DATE

CLICKS

SALES

NOTES

DESCRIPTION

FORMAT

START DATE

END DATE

CLICKS

SALES

NOTES

MONTH OF _____

Monday	Tuesday	Wednesday	Thursday	Friday	Saturday	Sunday

Awareness Goals:

_____

_____

_____

_____

Evaluation Goals:

_____

_____

_____

_____

Conversion & Retention Goals:

_____

_____

_____

_____

WEEK OF _____

Monday	Tuesday	Wednesday	Thursday	Friday	Saturday	Sunday

Awareness Goals:

_____
_____
_____
_____
_____

Evaluation Goals:

_____
_____
_____
_____
_____

Conversion & Retention Goals:

_____
_____
_____
_____
_____

WEEK OF _____

Monday	Tuesday	Wednesday	Thursday	Friday	Saturday	Sunday

Awareness Goals:

_____

_____

_____

_____

Evaluation Goals:

_____

_____

_____

_____

Conversion & Retention Goals:

_____

_____

_____

_____

WEEK OF _____

Monday	Tuesday	Wednesday	Thursday	Friday	Saturday	Sunday

Awareness Goals:

Evaluation Goals:

Conversion & Retention Goals:

WEEK OF

Monday	Tuesday	Wednesday	Thursday	Friday	Saturday	Sunday

Awareness Goals:

_____

_____

_____

_____

Evaluation Goals:

Conversion & Retention Goals:

_____

_____

_____

_____

WEEK OF _____

Monday	Tuesday	Wednesday	Thursday	Friday	Saturday	Sunday

Awareness Goals:

_____

_____

_____

_____

Evaluation Goals:

_____

_____

_____

_____

Conversion & Retention Goals:

_____

_____

_____

_____

DETAILED AD CAMPAIGN TRACKER

AD HEADLINE 1 _____

_____

AD HEADLINE 2 _____

_____

AD TEXT _____

_____

_____

_____

IMAGE IDEA _____

_____

URL _____

CALL TO ACTION
☐ SHOP NOW   ☐ DOWNLOAD   ☐ WATCH MORE   ☐ BOOK NOW
☐ LISTEN NOW   ☐ LEARN MORE   ☐ APPLY NOW   ☐ SIGN UP
☐ INSTALL NOW   ☐ DONATE NOW   ☐ USE APP   ☐ CONTACT US

AD TARGETS   AGE _____   LOCATION _____   GENDER _____

CUSTOM AUDIENCE _____   INTEREST _____

_____   _____

WHAT IS THE GOAL FOR THE AD?   ☐ AWARENESS   ☐ EVALUATION   ☐ CONVERSION

HOW WILL YOU TRACK SUCCESS? _____

_____

IS THE CALL TO ACTION CLEAR? ☐ YES ☐ NO   IS YOUR PIXEL INSTALLED? ☐ YES ☐ NO

AD BUDGET _____

AD DURATION _____

DETAILED AD CAMPAIGN TRACKER

AD HEADLINE 1 _____

_____

AD HEADLINE 2 _____

_____

AD TEXT _____

_____

_____

_____

IMAGE IDEA _____

_____

URL _____

CALL TO ACTION
☐ SHOP NOW ☐ DOWNLOAD ☐ WATCH MORE ☐ BOOK NOW
☐ LISTEN NOW ☐ LEARN MORE ☐ APPLY NOW ☐ SIGN UP
☐ INSTALL NOW ☐ DONATE NOW ☐ USE APP ☐ CONTACT US

AD TARGETS AGE _____ LOCATION _____ GENDER _____

CUSTOM AUDIENCE _____ INTEREST _____

_____ _____

WHAT IS THE GOAL FOR THE AD? ☐ AWARENESS ☐ EVALUATION ☐ CONVERSION

HOW WILL YOU TRACK SUCCESS? _____

_____

IS THE CALL TO ACTION CLEAR? ☐ YES ☐ NO   IS YOUR PIXEL INSTALLED? ☐ YES ☐ NO

AD BUDGET _____

AD DURATION _____ - _____

DETAILED AD CAMPAIGN TRACKER

AD HEADLINE 1 _____

_____

AD HEADLINE 2 _____

_____

AD TEXT _____

_____

_____

_____

IMAGE IDEA _____

_____

URL _____

CALL TO ACTION
- [ ] SHOP NOW
- [ ] DOWNLOAD
- [ ] WATCH MORE
- [ ] BOOK NOW
- [ ] LISTEN NOW
- [ ] LEARN MORE
- [ ] APPLY NOW
- [ ] SIGN UP
- [ ] INSTALL NOW
- [ ] DONATE NOW
- [ ] USE APP
- [ ] CONTACT US

AD TARGETS AGE _____ LOCATION _____ GENDER _____

CUSTOM AUDIENCE _____ INTEREST _____

_____ _____

WHAT IS THE GOAL FOR THE AD? [ ] AWARENESS [ ] EVALUATION [ ] CONVERSION

HOW WILL YOU TRACK SUCCESS? _____

_____

IS THE CALL TO ACTION CLEAR? [ ] YES [ ] NO   IS YOUR PIXEL INSTALLED? [ ] YES [ ] NO

AD BUDGET _____

AD DURATION _____ - _____

DETAILED AD CAMPAIGN TRACKER

AD HEADLINE 1

_____

_____

AD HEADLINE 2

_____

_____

AD TEXT

_____

_____

_____

_____

IMAGE IDEA

_____

_____

URL _____

CALL TO ACTION
- ☐ SHOP NOW ☐ DOWNLOAD ☐ WATCH MORE ☐ BOOK NOW
- ☐ LISTEN NOW ☐ LEARN MORE ☐ APPLY NOW ☐ SIGN UP
- ☐ INSTALL NOW ☐ DONATE NOW ☐ USE APP ☐ CONTACT US

AD TARGETS AGE _____ LOCATION _____ GENDER _____

CUSTOM AUDIENCE _____ INTEREST _____

_____ _____

WHAT IS THE GOAL FOR THE AD? ☐ AWARENESS ☐ EVALUATION ☐ CONVERSION

HOW WILL YOU TRACK SUCCESS? _____

_____

IS THE CALL TO ACTION CLEAR? ☐ YES ☐ NO   IS YOUR PIXEL INSTALLED? ☐ YES ☐ NO

AD BUDGET _____

AD DURATION _____ - _____

ADVERTISING TRACKER

DESCRIPTION

FORMAT

START DATE

END DATE

CLICKS

SALES

NOTES

DESCRIPTION

FORMAT

START DATE

END DATE

CLICKS

SALES

NOTES

ADVERTISING TRACKER

DESCRIPTION

FORMAT

START DATE

END DATE

CLICKS

SALES

NOTES

DESCRIPTION

FORMAT

START DATE

END DATE

CLICKS

SALES

NOTES

MONTH OF _____

Monday	Tuesday	Wednesday	Thursday	Friday	Saturday	Sunday

Awareness Goals:

_____

_____

_____

_____

Evaluation Goals:

_____

_____

_____

_____

Conversion & Retention Goals:

_____

_____

_____

_____

WEEK OF

Monday	Tuesday	Wednesday	Thursday	Friday	Saturday	Sunday

Awareness Goals:

_____
_____
_____

Evaluation Goals:

_____
_____
_____

Conversion & Retention Goals:

_____
_____
_____

WEEK OF

Monday	Tuesday	Wednesday	Thursday	Friday	Saturday	Sunday

Awareness Goals: _____

Evaluation Goals: _____

Conversion & Retention Goals: _____

WEEK OF _____

Monday	Tuesday	Wednesday	Thursday	Friday	Saturday	Sunday

Awareness Goals:

_____
_____
_____
_____

Evaluation Goals:

_____
_____
_____
_____

Conversion & Retention Goals:

_____
_____
_____
_____

WEEK OF

Monday	Tuesday	Wednesday	Thursday	Friday	Saturday	Sunday

Awareness Goals:

Evaluation Goals:

Conversion & Retention Goals:

WEEK OF

Monday	Tuesday	Wednesday	Thursday	Friday	Saturday	Sunday

Awareness Goals:

Evaluation Goals:

Conversion & Retention Goals:

DETAILED AD CAMPAIGN TRACKER

AD HEADLINE 1

_____

_____

AD HEADLINE 2

_____

_____

AD TEXT

_____

_____

_____

_____

_____

IMAGE IDEA

_____

_____

URL _____

CALL TO ACTION
☐ SHOP NOW ☐ DOWNLOAD ☐ WATCH MORE ☐ BOOK NOW
☐ LISTEN NOW ☐ LEARN MORE ☐ APPLY NOW ☐ SIGN UP
☐ INSTALL NOW ☐ DONATE NOW ☐ USE APP ☐ CONTACT US

AD TARGETS AGE _____ LOCATION _____ GENDER _____

CUSTOM AUDIENCE _____ INTEREST _____

_____ _____

WHAT IS THE GOAL FOR THE AD? ☐ AWARENESS ☐ EVALUATION ☐ CONVERSION

HOW WILL YOU TRACK SUCCESS? _____

_____

IS THE CALL TO ACTION CLEAR? ☐ YES ☐ NO   IS YOUR PIXEL INSTALLED? ☐ YES ☐ NO

AD BUDGET _____

AD DURATION _____ - _____

DETAILED AD CAMPAIGN TRACKER

AD HEADLINE 1 _____

_____

AD HEADLINE 2 _____

_____

AD TEXT _____

_____

_____

_____

_____

IMAGE IDEA _____

_____

URL _____

CALL TO ACTION
☐ SHOP NOW   ☐ DOWNLOAD   ☐ WATCH MORE   ☐ BOOK NOW
☐ LISTEN NOW   ☐ LEARN MORE   ☐ APPLY NOW   ☐ SIGN UP
☐ INSTALL NOW   ☐ DONATE NOW   ☐ USE APP   ☐ CONTACT US

AD TARGETS AGE _____ LOCATION _____ GENDER _____

CUSTOM AUDIENCE _____   INTEREST _____

_____   _____

WHAT IS THE GOAL FOR THE AD? ☐ AWARENESS ☐ EVALUATION ☐ CONVERSION

HOW WILL YOU TRACK SUCCESS? _____

_____

IS THE CALL TO ACTION CLEAR? ☐ YES ☐ NO   IS YOUR PIXEL INSTALLED? ☐ YES ☐ NO

AD BUDGET _____

AD DURATION _____ - _____

DETAILED AD CAMPAIGN TRACKER

AD HEADLINE 1 _____

_____

AD HEADLINE 2 _____

_____

AD TEXT _____

_____

_____

_____

IMAGE IDEA _____

_____

URL _____

CALL TO ACTION
☐ SHOP NOW   ☐ DOWNLOAD   ☐ WATCH MORE   ☐ BOOK NOW
☐ LISTEN NOW   ☐ LEARN MORE   ☐ APPLY NOW   ☐ SIGN UP
☐ INSTALL NOW   ☐ DONATE NOW   ☐ USE APP   ☐ CONTACT US

AD TARGETS   AGE _____   LOCATION _____   GENDER _____

CUSTOM AUDIENCE _____   INTEREST _____

_____   _____

WHAT IS THE GOAL FOR THE AD?   ☐ AWARENESS   ☐ EVALUATION   ☐ CONVERSION

HOW WILL YOU TRACK SUCCESS? _____

_____

IS THE CALL TO ACTION CLEAR?   ☐ YES ☐ NO   IS YOUR PIXEL INSTALLED?   ☐ YES ☐ NO

AD BUDGET _____

AD DURATION _____   -   _____

DETAILED AD CAMPAIGN TRACKER

AD HEADLINE 1 _____

_____

AD HEADLINE 2 _____

_____

AD TEXT _____

_____

_____

_____

IMAGE IDEA _____

_____

URL _____

CALL TO ACTION
- ☐ SHOP NOW ☐ DOWNLOAD ☐ WATCH MORE ☐ BOOK NOW
- ☐ LISTEN NOW ☐ LEARN MORE ☐ APPLY NOW ☐ SIGN UP
- ☐ INSTALL NOW ☐ DONATE NOW ☐ USE APP ☐ CONTACT US

AD TARGETS AGE _____ LOCATION _____ GENDER _____

CUSTOM AUDIENCE _____ INTEREST _____

_____ _____

WHAT IS THE GOAL FOR THE AD? ☐ AWARENESS ☐ EVALUATION ☐ CONVERSION

HOW WILL YOU TRACK SUCCESS? _____

_____

IS THE CALL TO ACTION CLEAR? ☐ YES ☐ NO   IS YOUR PIXEL INSTALLED? ☐ YES ☐ NO

AD BUDGET _____

AD DURATION _____ - _____

ADVERTISING TRACKER

DESCRIPTION

FORMAT

START DATE

END DATE

CLICKS

SALES

NOTES

DESCRIPTION

FORMAT

START DATE

END DATE

CLICKS

SALES

NOTES

ADVERTISING TRACKER

DESCRIPTION

FORMAT

START DATE

END DATE

CLICKS

SALES

NOTES

DESCRIPTION

FORMAT

START DATE

END DATE

CLICKS

SALES

NOTES

MONTH OF _____

Monday	Tuesday	Wednesday	Thursday	Friday	Saturday	Sunday

Awareness Goals:

_____

_____

_____

_____

Evaluation Goals:

_____

_____

_____

_____

Conversion & Retention Goals:

_____

_____

_____

_____

WEEK OF _____

Monday	Tuesday	Wednesday	Thursday	Friday	Saturday	Sunday

Awareness Goals:

_____

_____

_____

_____

Evaluation Goals:

_____

_____

_____

_____

Conversion & Retention Goals:

_____

_____

_____

_____

WEEK OF

Monday	Tuesday	Wednesday	Thursday	Friday	Saturday	Sunday

Awareness Goals:

Evaluation Goals:

Conversion & Retention Goals:

WEEK OF _____

Monday	Tuesday	Wednesday	Thursday	Friday	Saturday	Sunday

Awareness Goals:

_____
_____
_____
_____

Evaluation Goals:

_____
_____
_____
_____

Conversion & Retention Goals:

_____
_____
_____
_____

WEEK OF

Monday	Tuesday	Wednesday	Thursday	Friday	Saturday	Sunday

Awareness Goals:

Evaluation Goals:

Conversion & Retention Goals:

WEEK OF _____

Monday	Tuesday	Wednesday	Thursday	Friday	Saturday	Sunday

Awareness Goals:

_____

_____

_____

_____

Evaluation Goals:

_____

_____

_____

_____

Conversion & Retention Goals:

_____

_____

_____

_____

DETAILED AD CAMPAIGN TRACKER

AD HEADLINE 1 _____

_____

AD HEADLINE 2 _____

_____

AD TEXT _____

_____

_____

_____

IMAGE IDEA _____

_____

URL _____

CALL TO ACTION
- [ ] SHOP NOW - [ ] DOWNLOAD - [ ] WATCH MORE - [ ] BOOK NOW
- [ ] LISTEN NOW - [ ] LEARN MORE - [ ] APPLY NOW - [ ] SIGN UP
- [ ] INSTALL NOW - [ ] DONATE NOW - [ ] USE APP - [ ] CONTACT US

AD TARGETS AGE _____ LOCATION _____ GENDER _____

CUSTOM AUDIENCE _____ INTEREST _____

_____

WHAT IS THE GOAL FOR THE AD? - [ ] AWARENESS - [ ] EVALUATION - [ ] CONVERSION

HOW WILL YOU TRACK SUCCESS? _____

_____

IS THE CALL TO ACTION CLEAR? - [ ] YES - [ ] NO   IS YOUR PIXEL INSTALLED? - [ ] YES - [ ] NO

AD BUDGET _____

AD DURATION _____

DETAILED AD CAMPAIGN TRACKER

AD HEADLINE 1

_____

_____

AD HEADLINE 2

_____

_____

AD TEXT

_____

_____

_____

_____

IMAGE IDEA

_____

_____

URL _____

CALL TO ACTION
- ☐ SHOP NOW
- ☐ DOWNLOAD
- ☐ WATCH MORE
- ☐ BOOK NOW
- ☐ LISTEN NOW
- ☐ LEARN MORE
- ☐ APPLY NOW
- ☐ SIGN UP
- ☐ INSTALL NOW
- ☐ DONATE NOW
- ☐ USE APP
- ☐ CONTACT US

AD TARGETS AGE _____ LOCATION _____ GENDER _____

CUSTOM AUDIENCE _____ INTEREST _____

_____ _____

WHAT IS THE GOAL FOR THE AD? ☐ AWARENESS ☐ EVALUATION ☐ CONVERSION

HOW WILL YOU TRACK SUCCESS? _____

_____

IS THE CALL TO ACTION CLEAR? ☐ YES ☐ NO   IS YOUR PIXEL INSTALLED? ☐ YES ☐ NO

AD BUDGET _____

AD DURATION _____

DETAILED AD CAMPAIGN TRACKER

AD HEADLINE 1 _____

_____

AD HEADLINE 2 _____

_____

AD TEXT _____

_____

_____

_____

IMAGE IDEA _____

_____

URL _____

CALL TO ACTION
☐ SHOP NOW ☐ DOWNLOAD ☐ WATCH MORE ☐ BOOK NOW
☐ LISTEN NOW ☐ LEARN MORE ☐ APPLY NOW ☐ SIGN UP
☐ INSTALL NOW ☐ DONATE NOW ☐ USE APP ☐ CONTACT US

AD TARGETS AGE _____ LOCATION _____ GENDER _____

CUSTOM AUDIENCE _____ INTEREST _____

_____ _____

WHAT IS THE GOAL FOR THE AD? ☐ AWARENESS ☐ EVALUATION ☐ CONVERSION

HOW WILL YOU TRACK SUCCESS? _____

_____

IS THE CALL TO ACTION CLEAR? ☐ YES ☐ NO   IS YOUR PIXEL INSTALLED? ☐ YES ☐ NO

AD BUDGET _____

AD DURATION _____ - _____

DETAILED AD CAMPAIGN TRACKER

AD HEADLINE 1 _____

_____

AD HEADLINE 2 _____

_____

AD TEXT _____

_____

_____

_____

IMAGE IDEA _____

_____

URL _____

CALL TO ACTION
- ☐ SHOP NOW   ☐ DOWNLOAD   ☐ WATCH MORE   ☐ BOOK NOW
- ☐ LISTEN NOW   ☐ LEARN MORE   ☐ APPLY NOW   ☐ SIGN UP
- ☐ INSTALL NOW   ☐ DONATE NOW   ☐ USE APP   ☐ CONTACT US

AD TARGETS   AGE _____   LOCATION _____   GENDER _____

CUSTOM AUDIENCE _____   INTEREST _____

_____   _____

WHAT IS THE GOAL FOR THE AD?   ☐ AWARENESS   ☐ EVALUATION   ☐ CONVERSION

HOW WILL YOU TRACK SUCCESS? _____

_____

IS THE CALL TO ACTION CLEAR? ☐ YES ☐ NO   IS YOUR PIXEL INSTALLED? ☐ YES ☐ NO

AD BUDGET _____

AD DURATION _____ - _____

ADVERTISING TRACKER

DESCRIPTION

FORMAT

START DATE

END DATE

CLICKS

SALES

NOTES

DESCRIPTION

FORMAT

START DATE

END DATE

CLICKS

SALES

NOTES

ADVERTISING TRACKER

DESCRIPTION

FORMAT

START DATE

END DATE

CLICKS

SALES

NOTES

DESCRIPTION

FORMAT

START DATE

END DATE

CLICKS

SALES

NOTES

MONTH OF _____

Monday	Tuesday	Wednesday	Thursday	Friday	Saturday	Sunday

Awareness Goals:

_____
_____
_____
_____

Evaluation Goals:

_____
_____
_____
_____

Conversion & Retention Goals:

_____
_____
_____
_____

WEEK OF _____

Monday	Tuesday	Wednesday	Thursday	Friday	Saturday	Sunday

Awareness Goals:

_____

_____

_____

_____

Evaluation Goals:

_____

_____

_____

_____

Conversion & Retention Goals:

_____

_____

_____

_____

WEEK OF

Monday	Tuesday	Wednesday	Thursday	Friday	Saturday	Sunday

Awareness Goals:

Evaluation Goals:

Conversion & Retention Goals:

WEEK OF _____

Monday	Tuesday	Wednesday	Thursday	Friday	Saturday	Sunday

Awareness Goals:

_____
_____
_____
_____

Evaluation Goals:

_____
_____
_____
_____

Conversion & Retention Goals:

_____
_____
_____
_____

WEEK OF

Monday	Tuesday	Wednesday	Thursday	Friday	Saturday	Sunday

Awareness Goals:

Evaluation Goals:

Conversion & Retention Goals:

WEEK OF _____

Monday	Tuesday	Wednesday	Thursday	Friday	Saturday	Sunday

Awareness Goals:
_____
_____
_____
_____

Evaluation Goals:
_____
_____
_____
_____

Conversion & Retention Goals:
_____
_____
_____
_____

DETAILED AD CAMPAIGN TRACKER

AD HEADLINE 1

_____

_____

AD HEADLINE 2

_____

_____

AD TEXT

_____

_____

_____

_____

IMAGE IDEA

_____

_____

URL _____

CALL TO ACTION   ☐ SHOP NOW   ☐ DOWNLOAD   ☐ WATCH MORE   ☐ BOOK NOW

☐ LISTEN NOW   ☐ LEARN MORE   ☐ APPLY NOW   ☐ SIGN UP

☐ INSTALL NOW   ☐ DONATE NOW   ☐ USE APP   ☐ CONTACT US

AD TARGETS   AGE _____   LOCATION _____   GENDER _____

CUSTOM AUDIENCE _____   INTEREST _____

_____   _____

WHAT IS THE GOAL FOR THE AD?   ☐ AWARENESS   ☐ EVALUATION   ☐ CONVERSION

HOW WILL YOU TRACK SUCCESS? _____

_____

IS THE CALL TO ACTION CLEAR? ☐ YES ☐ NO   IS YOUR PIXEL INSTALLED? ☐ YES ☐ NO

AD BUDGET _____

AD DURATION _____ - _____

DETAILED AD CAMPAIGN TRACKER

AD HEADLINE 1

_____

_____

AD HEADLINE 2

_____

_____

AD TEXT

_____

_____

_____

_____

IMAGE IDEA

_____

_____

URL _____

CALL TO ACTION
- [ ] SHOP NOW
- [ ] DOWNLOAD
- [ ] WATCH MORE
- [ ] BOOK NOW
- [ ] LISTEN NOW
- [ ] LEARN MORE
- [ ] APPLY NOW
- [ ] SIGN UP
- [ ] INSTALL NOW
- [ ] DONATE NOW
- [ ] USE APP
- [ ] CONTACT US

AD TARGETS AGE _____ LOCATION _____ GENDER _____

CUSTOM AUDIENCE _____ INTEREST _____

_____

WHAT IS THE GOAL FOR THE AD? [ ] AWARENESS [ ] EVALUATION [ ] CONVERSION

HOW WILL YOU TRACK SUCCESS? _____

_____

IS THE CALL TO ACTION CLEAR? [ ] YES [ ] NO   IS YOUR PIXEL INSTALLED? [ ] YES [ ] NO

AD BUDGET _____

AD DURATION _____ - _____

DETAILED AD CAMPAIGN TRACKER

AD HEADLINE 1

_____

_____

AD HEADLINE 2

_____

_____

AD TEXT

_____

_____

_____

_____

IMAGE IDEA

_____

_____

URL _____

CALL TO ACTION
☐ SHOP NOW ☐ DOWNLOAD ☐ WATCH MORE ☐ BOOK NOW

☐ LISTEN NOW ☐ LEARN MORE ☐ APPLY NOW ☐ SIGN UP

☐ INSTALL NOW ☐ DONATE NOW ☐ USE APP ☐ CONTACT US

AD TARGETS AGE _____ LOCATION _____ GENDER _____

CUSTOM AUDIENCE _____ INTEREST _____

_____ _____

WHAT IS THE GOAL FOR THE AD? ☐ AWARENESS ☐ EVALUATION ☐ CONVERSION

HOW WILL YOU TRACK SUCCESS? _____

_____

IS THE CALL TO ACTION CLEAR? ☐ YES ☐ NO   IS YOUR PIXEL INSTALLED? ☐ YES ☐ NO

AD BUDGET _____

AD DURATION _____ - _____

DETAILED AD CAMPAIGN TRACKER

AD HEADLINE 1 _____

_____

AD HEADLINE 2 _____

_____

AD TEXT _____

_____

_____

_____

IMAGE IDEA _____

_____

URL _____

CALL TO ACTION
☐ SHOP NOW ☐ DOWNLOAD ☐ WATCH MORE ☐ BOOK NOW
☐ LISTEN NOW ☐ LEARN MORE ☐ APPLY NOW ☐ SIGN UP
☐ INSTALL NOW ☐ DONATE NOW ☐ USE APP ☐ CONTACT US

AD TARGETS AGE _____ LOCATION _____ GENDER _____

CUSTOM AUDIENCE _____ INTEREST _____

_____ _____

WHAT IS THE GOAL FOR THE AD? ☐ AWARENESS ☐ EVALUATION ☐ CONVERSION

HOW WILL YOU TRACK SUCCESS? _____

_____

IS THE CALL TO ACTION CLEAR? ☐ YES ☐ NO   IS YOUR PIXEL INSTALLED? ☐ YES ☐ NO

AD BUDGET _____

AD DURATION _____ - _____

ADVERTISING TRACKER

DESCRIPTION

FORMAT

START DATE

END DATE

CLICKS

SALES

NOTES

DESCRIPTION

FORMAT

START DATE

END DATE

CLICKS

SALES

NOTES

ADVERTISING TRACKER

DESCRIPTION

FORMAT

START DATE

END DATE

CLICKS

SALES

NOTES

DESCRIPTION

FORMAT

START DATE

END DATE

CLICKS

SALES

NOTES

MONTH OF _____

Monday	Tuesday	Wednesday	Thursday	Friday	Saturday	Sunday

Awareness Goals:

_____
_____
_____
_____

Evaluation Goals:

_____
_____
_____
_____

Conversion & Retention Goals:

_____
_____
_____
_____

WEEK OF _____

Monday	Tuesday	Wednesday	Thursday	Friday	Saturday	Sunday

Awareness Goals:

_____

_____

_____

_____

Evaluation Goals:

_____

_____

_____

_____

Conversion & Retention Goals:

_____

_____

_____

_____

WEEK OF

Monday	Tuesday	Wednesday	Thursday	Friday	Saturday	Sunday

Awareness Goals:

_____

_____

_____

_____

Evaluation Goals:

_____

_____

_____

_____

Conversion & Retention Goals:

_____

_____

_____

_____

WEEK OF _____

Monday	Tuesday	Wednesday	Thursday	Friday	Saturday	Sunday

Awareness Goals:

_____

_____

_____

Evaluation Goals:

_____

_____

_____

Conversion & Retention Goals:

_____

_____

_____

WEEK OF

Monday	Tuesday	Wednesday	Thursday	Friday	Saturday	Sunday

Awareness Goals:

_____

_____

_____

_____

Evaluation Goals:

_____

_____

_____

_____

Conversion & Retention Goals:

_____

_____

_____

_____

WEEK OF

Monday	Tuesday	Wednesday	Thursday	Friday	Saturday	Sunday

Awareness Goals:

_____

_____

Evaluation Goals:

_____

_____

_____

Conversion & Retention Goals:

_____

_____

_____

DETAILED AD CAMPAIGN TRACKER

AD HEADLINE 1 _____

_____

AD HEADLINE 2 _____

_____

AD TEXT _____

_____

_____

_____

IMAGE IDEA _____

_____

URL _____

CALL TO ACTION
- ☐ SHOP NOW
- ☐ DOWNLOAD
- ☐ WATCH MORE
- ☐ BOOK NOW
- ☐ LISTEN NOW
- ☐ LEARN MORE
- ☐ APPLY NOW
- ☐ SIGN UP
- ☐ INSTALL NOW
- ☐ DONATE NOW
- ☐ USE APP
- ☐ CONTACT US

AD TARGETS AGE _____ LOCATION _____ GENDER _____

CUSTOM AUDIENCE _____ INTEREST _____

_____ _____

WHAT IS THE GOAL FOR THE AU? ☐ AWARENESS ☐ EVALUATION ☐ CONVERSION

HOW WILL YOU TRACK SUCCESS? _____

_____

IS THE CALL TO ACTION CLEAR? ☐ YES ☐ NO   IS YOUR PIXEL INSTALLED? ☐ YES ☐ NO

AD BUDGET _____

AD DURATION _____ - _____

DETAILED AD CAMPAIGN TRACKER

AD HEADLINE 1

_____

_____

AD HEADLINE 2

_____

_____

AD TEXT

_____

_____

_____

_____

IMAGE IDEA

_____

_____

URL _____

CALL TO ACTION
- ☐ SHOP NOW   ☐ DOWNLOAD   ☐ WATCH MORE   ☐ BOOK NOW
- ☐ LISTEN NOW   ☐ LEARN MORE   ☐ APPLY NOW   ☐ SIGN UP
- ☐ INSTALL NOW   ☐ DONATE NOW   ☐ USE APP   ☐ CONTACT US

AD TARGETS AGE _____ LOCATION _____ GENDER _____

CUSTOM AUDIENCE _____ INTEREST _____

_____   _____

WHAT IS THE GOAL FOR THE AD? ☐ AWARENESS ☐ EVALUATION ☐ CONVERSION

HOW WILL YOU TRACK SUCCESS? _____

_____

IS THE CALL TO ACTION CLEAR? ☐ YES ☐ NO   IS YOUR PIXEL INSTALLED? ☐ YES ☐ NO

AD BUDGET _____

AD DURATION _____ - _____

DETAILED AD CAMPAIGN TRACKER

AD HEADLINE 1 _____

_____

AD HEADLINE 2 _____

_____

AD TEXT _____

_____

_____

_____

IMAGE IDEA _____

_____

URL _____

CALL TO ACTION
☐ SHOP NOW   ☐ DOWNLOAD   ☐ WATCH MORE   ☐ BOOK NOW
☐ LISTEN NOW   ☐ LEARN MORE   ☐ APPLY NOW   ☐ SIGN UP
☐ INSTALL NOW   ☐ DONATE NOW   ☐ USE APP   ☐ CONTACT US

AD TARGETS AGE _____ LOCATION _____ GENDER _____

CUSTOM AUDIENCE _____   INTEREST _____

_____   _____

WHAT IS THE GOAL FOR THE AD? ☐ AWARENESS ☐ EVALUATION ☐ CONVERSION

HOW WILL YOU TRACK SUCCESS? _____

_____

IS THE CALL TO ACTION CLEAR? ☐ YES ☐ NO   IS YOUR PIXEL INSTALLED? ☐ YES ☐ NO

AD BUDGET _____

AD DURATION _____ - _____

DETAILED AD CAMPAIGN TRACKER

AD HEADLINE 1 _____

_____

AD HEADLINE 2 _____

_____

AD TEXT _____

_____

_____

_____

IMAGE IDEA _____

_____

URL _____

CALL TO ACTION
☐ SHOP NOW ☐ DOWNLOAD ☐ WATCH MORE ☐ BOOK NOW
☐ LISTEN NOW ☐ LEARN MORE ☐ APPLY NOW ☐ SIGN UP
☐ INSTALL NOW ☐ DONATE NOW ☐ USE APP ☐ CONTACT US

AD TARGETS AGE _____ LOCATION _____ GENDER _____

CUSTOM AUDIENCE _____ INTEREST _____

_____ _____

WHAT IS THE GOAL FOR THE AD? ☐ AWARENESS ☐ EVALUATION ☐ CONVERSION

HOW WILL YOU TRACK SUCCESS? _____

_____

IS THE CALL TO ACTION CLEAR? ☐ YES ☐ NO   IS YOUR PIXEL INSTALLED? ☐ YES ☐ NO

AD BUDGET _____

AD DURATION _____ - _____

ADVERTISING TRACKER

DESCRIPTION

FORMAT

START DATE

END DATE

CLICKS

SALES

NOTES

DESCRIPTION

FORMAT

START DATE

END DATE

CLICKS

SALES

NOTES

ADVERTISING TRACKER

DESCRIPTION

FORMAT

START DATE

END DATE

CLICKS

SALES

NOTES

DESCRIPTION

FORMAT

START DATE

END DATE

CLICKS

SALES

NOTES

MONTH OF _____

Monday	Tuesday	Wednesday	Thursday	Friday	Saturday	Sunday

Awareness Goals:

_____

_____

_____

_____

Evaluation Goals:

_____

_____

_____

_____

Conversion & Retention Goals:

_____

_____

_____

_____

WEEK OF _____

Monday	Tuesday	Wednesday	Thursday	Friday	Saturday	Sunday

Awareness Goals:

_____
_____
_____
_____

Evaluation Goals:

_____
_____
_____
_____

Conversion & Retention Goals:

_____
_____
_____
_____

WEEK OF

Monday	Tuesday	Wednesday	Thursday	Friday	Saturday	Sunday

Awareness Goals:

_____
_____
_____
_____

Evaluation Goals:

_____
_____
_____
_____

Conversion & Retention Goals:

_____
_____
_____
_____

WEEK OF _____

Monday	Tuesday	Wednesday	Thursday	Friday	Saturday	Sunday

Awareness Goals:

Evaluation Goals:

Conversion & Retention Goals:

WEEK OF _____

Monday	
Tuesday	
Wednesday	
Thursday	
Friday	
Saturday	
Sunday	

Awareness Goals:

_____

_____

_____

_____

Evaluation Goals:

_____

_____

_____

_____

Conversion & Retention Goals:

_____

_____

_____

_____

WEEK OF _____

Monday	Tuesday	Wednesday	Thursday	Friday	Saturday	Sunday

Awareness Goals:

_____

_____

_____

Evaluation Goals:

_____

_____

_____

Conversion & Retention Goals:

_____

_____

_____

DETAILED AD CAMPAIGN TRACKER

AD HEADLINE 1 _____

_____

AD HEADLINE 2 _____

_____

AD TEXT _____

_____

_____

_____

IMAGE IDEA _____

_____

URL _____

CALL TO ACTION
☐ SHOP NOW ☐ DOWNLOAD ☐ WATCH MORE ☐ BOOK NOW
☐ LISTEN NOW ☐ LEARN MORE ☐ APPLY NOW ☐ SIGN UP
☐ INSTALL NOW ☐ DONATE NOW ☐ USE APP ☐ CONTACT US

AD TARGETS AGE _____ LOCATION _____ GENDER _____

CUSTOM AUDIENCE _____ INTEREST _____

_____ _____

WHAT IS THE GOAL FOR THE AD? ☐ AWARENESS ☐ EVALUATION ☐ CONVERSION

HOW WILL YOU TRACK SUCCESS? _____

_____

IS THE CALL TO ACTION CLEAR? ☐ YES ☐ NO   IS YOUR PIXEL INSTALLED? ☐ YES ☐ NO

AD BUDGET _____

AD DURATION _____ - _____

DETAILED AD CAMPAIGN TRACKER

AD HEADLINE 1

_____

_____

AD HEADLINE 2

_____

_____

AD TEXT

_____

_____

_____

_____

IMAGE IDEA

_____

_____

URL _____

CALL TO ACTION
- ☐ SHOP NOW ☐ DOWNLOAD ☐ WATCH MORE ☐ BOOK NOW
- ☐ LISTEN NOW ☐ LEARN MORE ☐ APPLY NOW ☐ SIGN UP
- ☐ INSTALL NOW ☐ DONATE NOW ☐ USE APP ☐ CONTACT US

AD TARGETS AGE _____ LOCATION _____ GENDER _____

CUSTOM AUDIENCE _____ INTEREST _____

_____ _____

WHAT IS THE GOAL FOR THE AD? ☐ AWARENESS ☐ EVALUATION ☐ CONVERSION

HOW WILL YOU TRACK SUCCESS? _____

_____

IS THE CALL TO ACTION CLEAR? ☐ YES ☐ NO   IS YOUR PIXEL INSTALLED? ☐ YES ☐ NO

AD BUDGET _____

AD DURATION _____

DETAILED AD CAMPAIGN TRACKER

AD HEADLINE 1 _____

_____

AD HEADLINE 2 _____

_____

AD TEXT _____

_____

_____

_____

IMAGE IDEA _____

_____

URL _____

CALL TO ACTION   ☐ SHOP NOW   ☐ DOWNLOAD   ☐ WATCH MORE   ☐ BOOK NOW

☐ LISTEN NOW   ☐ LEARN MORE   ☐ APPLY NOW   ☐ SIGN UP

☐ INSTALL NOW   ☐ DONATE NOW   ☐ USE APP   ☐ CONTACT US

AD TARGETS   AGE _____   LOCATION _____   GENDER _____

CUSTOM AUDIENCE _____   INTEREST _____

_____   _____

WHAT IS THE GOAL FOR THE AD?   ☐ AWARENESS   ☐ EVALUATION   ☐ CONVERSION

HOW WILL YOU TRACK SUCCESS? _____

_____

IS THE CALL TO ACTION CLEAR?   ☐ YES   ☐ NO   IS YOUR PIXEL INSTALLED?   ☐ YES   ☐ NO

AD BUDGET _____

AD DURATION _____ - _____

DETAILED AD CAMPAIGN TRACKER

AD HEADLINE 1

_____

_____

AD HEADLINE 2

_____

_____

AD TEXT

_____

_____

_____

_____

IMAGE IDEA

_____

_____

URL _____

CALL TO ACTION
☐ SHOP NOW ☐ DOWNLOAD ☐ WATCH MORE ☐ BOOK NOW
☐ LISTEN NOW ☐ LEARN MORE ☐ APPLY NOW ☐ SIGN UP
☐ INSTALL NOW ☐ DONATE NOW ☐ USE APP ☐ CONTACT US

AD TARGETS AGE _____ LOCATION _____ GENDER _____

CUSTOM AUDIENCE _____ INTEREST _____

_____   _____

WHAT IS THE GOAL FOR THE AD? ☐ AWARENESS ☐ EVALUATION ☐ CONVERSION

HOW WILL YOU TRACK SUCCESS? _____

_____

IS THE CALL TO ACTION CLEAR? ☐ YES ☐ NO   IS YOUR PIXEL INSTALLED? ☐ YES ☐ NO

AD BUDGET _____

AD DURATION _____ - _____

ADVERTISING TRACKER

DESCRIPTION

FORMAT

START DATE

END DATE

CLICKS

SALES

NOTES

DESCRIPTION

FORMAT

START DATE

END DATE

CLICKS

SALES

NOTES

ADVERTISING TRACKER

DESCRIPTION

FORMAT

START DATE

END DATE

CLICKS

SALES

NOTES

DESCRIPTION

FORMAT

START DATE

END DATE

CLICKS

SALES

NOTES

MONTH OF _____

Monday	Tuesday	Wednesday	Thursday	Friday	Saturday	Sunday

Awareness Goals:

_____
_____
_____
_____

Evaluation Goals:

_____
_____
_____
_____

Conversion & Retention Goals:

_____
_____
_____
_____

WEEK OF _____

Monday	Tuesday	Wednesday	Thursday	Friday	Saturday	Sunday

Awareness Goals:

_____

_____

_____

_____

Evaluation Goals:

_____

_____

_____

_____

Conversion & Retention Goals:

_____

_____

_____

_____

WEEK OF

Monday	Tuesday	Wednesday	Thursday	Friday	Saturday	Sunday

Awareness Goals:

_____

_____

_____

_____

Evaluation Goals:

_____

_____

_____

_____

Corversion & Retention Goals:

_____

_____

_____

_____

WEEK OF _____

Monday	Tuesday	Wednesday	Thursday	Friday	Saturday	Sunday

Awareness Goals:

_____

_____

_____

_____

Evaluation Goals:

_____

_____

_____

_____

Conversion & Retention Goals:

_____

_____

_____

_____

WEEK OF _____

Monday	Tuesday	Wednesday	Thursday	Friday	Saturday	Sunday

Awareness Goals:

_____

_____

_____

_____

Evaluation Goals:

_____

_____

_____

_____

Conversion & Retention Goals:

_____

_____

_____

_____

WEEK OF _____

Monday	Tuesday	Wednesday	Thursday	Friday	Saturday	Sunday

Awareness Goals:

Evaluation Goals:

Conversion & Retention Goals:

DETAILED AD CAMPAIGN TRACKER

AD HEADLINE 1 _____

_____

AD HEADLINE 2 _____

_____

AD TEXT _____

_____

_____

_____

IMAGE IDEA _____

_____

URL _____

CALL TO ACTION
- ☐ SHOP NOW
- ☐ DOWNLOAD
- ☐ WATCH MORE
- ☐ BOOK NOW
- ☐ LISTEN NOW
- ☐ LEARN MORE
- ☐ APPLY NOW
- ☐ SIGN UP
- ☐ INSTALL NOW
- ☐ DONATE NOW
- ☐ USE APP
- ☐ CONTACT US

AD TARGETS AGE _____ LOCATION _____ GENDER _____

CUSTOM AUDIENCE _____ INTEREST _____

_____

WHAT IS THE GOAL FOR THE AD? ☐ AWARENESS ☐ EVALUATION ☐ CONVERSION

HOW WILL YOU TRACK SUCCESS? _____

_____

IS THE CALL TO ACTION CLEAR? ☐ YES ☐ NO   IS YOUR PIXEL INSTALLED? ☐ YES ☐ NO

AD BUDGET _____

AD DURATION _____

DETAILED AD CAMPAIGN TRACKER

AD HEADLINE 1 _____

_____

AD HEADLINE 2 _____

_____

AD TEXT _____

_____

_____

_____

IMAGE IDEA _____

_____

URL _____

CALL TO ACTION
☐ SHOP NOW   ☐ DOWNLOAD   ☐ WATCH MORE   ☐ BOOK NOW

☐ LISTEN NOW   ☐ LEARN MORE   ☐ APPLY NOW   ☐ SIGN UP

☐ INSTALL NOW   ☐ DONATE NOW   ☐ USE APP   ☐ CONTACT US

AD TARGETS   AGE _____   LOCATION _____   GENDER _____

CUSTOM AUDIENCE _____   INTEREST _____

_____   _____

WHAT IS THE GOAL FOR THE AD?   ☐ AWARENESS   ☐ EVALUATION   ☐ CONVERSION

HOW WILL YOU TRACK SUCCESS? _____

_____

IS THE CALL TO ACTION CLEAR? ☐ YES ☐ NO   IS YOUR PIXEL INSTALLED? ☐ YES ☐ NO

AD BUDGET _____

AD DURATION _____ - _____

DETAILED AD CAMPAIGN TRACKER

AD HEADLINE 1 _____

_____

AD HEADLINE 2 _____

_____

AD TEXT _____

_____

_____

_____

IMAGE IDEA _____

_____

URL _____

CALL TO ACTION
☐ SHOP NOW ☐ DOWNLOAD ☐ WATCH MORE ☐ BOOK NOW
☐ LISTEN NOW ☐ LEARN MORE ☐ APPLY NOW ☐ SIGN UP
☐ INSTALL NOW ☐ DONATE NOW ☐ USE APP ☐ CONTACT US

AD TARGETS AGE _____ LOCATION _____ GENDER _____

CUSTOM AUDIENCE _____ INTEREST _____

_____   _____

WHAT IS THE GOAL FOR THE AD? ☐ AWARENESS ☐ EVALUATION ☐ CONVERSION

HOW WILL YOU TRACK SUCCESS? _____

_____

IS THE CALL TO ACTION CLEAR? ☐ YES ☐ NO   IS YOUR PIXEL INSTALLED? ☐ YES ☐ NO

AD BUDGET _____

AD DURATION _____ - _____

DETAILED AD CAMPAIGN TRACKER

AD HEADLINE 1
_____

_____

AD HEADLINE 2
_____

_____

AD TEXT
_____

_____

_____

_____

IMAGE IDEA
_____

_____

URL _____

CALL TO ACTION
☐ SHOP NOW ☐ DOWNLOAD ☐ WATCH MORE ☐ BOOK NOW

☐ LISTEN NOW ☐ LEARN MORE ☐ APPLY NOW ☐ SIGN UP

☐ INSTALL NOW ☐ DONATE NOW ☐ USE APP ☐ CONTACT US

AD TARGETS AGE _____ LOCATION _____ GENDER _____

CUSTOM AUDIENCE _____ INTEREST _____

_____ _____

WHAT IS THE GOAL FOR THE AD? ☐ AWARENESS ☐ EVALUATION ☐ CONVERSION

HOW WILL YOU TRACK SUCCESS? _____

_____

IS THE CALL TO ACTION CLEAR? ☐ YES ☐ NO   IS YOUR PIXEL INSTALLED? ☐ YES ☐ NO

AD BUDGET _____

AD DURATION _____

ADVERTISING TRACKER

DESCRIPTION

FORMAT

START DATE

END DATE

CLICKS

SALES

NOTES

DESCRIPTION

FORMAT

START DATE

END DATE

CLICKS

SALES

NOTES

ADVERTISING TRACKER

DESCRIPTION

FORMAT

START DATE

END DATE

CLICKS

SALES

NOTES

DESCRIPTION

FORMAT

START DATE

END DATE

CLICKS

SALES

NOTES

MONTH OF _____

Monday	Tuesday	Wednesday	Thursday	Friday	Saturday	Sunday

Awareness Goals:

_____

_____

_____

_____

_____

Evaluation Goals:

_____

_____

_____

_____

_____

Conversion & Retention Goals:

_____

_____

_____

_____

_____

WEEK OF _____

Monday	Tuesday	Wednesday	Thursday	Friday	Saturday	Sunday

Awareness Goals:

_____
_____
_____
_____

Evaluation Goals:

_____
_____
_____
_____

Conversion & Retention Goals:

_____
_____
_____
_____

WEEK OF

Monday	Tuesday	Wednesday	Thursday	Friday	Saturday	Sunday

Awareness Goals:

Evaluation Goals:

Conversion & Retention Goals:

WEEK OF _____

Monday	Tuesday	Wednesday	Thursday	Friday	Saturday	Sunday

Awareness Goals:

Evaluation Goals:

Conversion & Retention Goals:

WEEK OF

Monday	Tuesday	Wednesday	Thursday	Friday	Saturday	Sunday

Awareness Goals:

Evaluation Goals:

Conversion & Retention Goals:

WEEK OF _____

Monday	Tuesday	Wednesday	Thursday	Friday	Saturday	Sunday

Awareness Goals:

_____
_____
_____

Evaluation Goals:

_____
_____
_____

Conversion & Retention Goals:

_____
_____
_____
_____

DETAILED AD CAMPAIGN TRACKER

AD HEADLINE 1

_____

_____

AD HEADLINE 2

_____

_____

AD TEXT

_____

_____

_____

_____

IMAGE IDEA

_____

_____

URL _____

CALL TO ACTION
- ☐ SHOP NOW ☐ DOWNLOAD ☐ WATCH MORE ☐ BOOK NOW
- ☐ LISTEN NOW ☐ LEARN MORE ☐ APPLY NOW ☐ SIGN UP
- ☐ INSTALL NOW ☐ DONATE NOW ☐ USE APP ☐ CONTACT US

AD TARGETS AGE _____ LOCATION _____ GENDER _____

CUSTOM AUDIENCE _____ INTEREST _____

_____ _____

WHAT IS THE GOAL FOR THE AD? ☐ AWARENESS ☐ EVALUATION ☐ CONVERSION

HOW WILL YOU TRACK SUCCESS? _____

_____

IS THE CALL TO ACTION CLEAR? ☐ YES ☐ NO   IS YOUR PIXEL INSTALLED? ☐ YES ☐ NO

AD BUDGET _____

AD DURATION _____ - _____

DETAILED AD CAMPAIGN TRACKER

AD HEADLINE 1
_____
_____

AD HEADLINE 2
_____
_____

AD TEXT
_____
_____
_____
_____

IMAGE IDEA
_____
_____

URL
_____

CALL TO ACTION
☐ SHOP NOW ☐ DOWNLOAD ☐ WATCH MORE ☐ BOOK NOW
☐ LISTEN NOW ☐ LEARN MORE ☐ APPLY NOW ☐ SIGN UP
☐ INSTALL NOW ☐ DONATE NOW ☐ USE APP ☐ CONTACT US

AD TARGETS AGE _____ LOCATION _____ GENDER _____

CUSTOM AUDIENCE _____ INTEREST _____
_____

WHAT IS THE GOAL FOR THE AD? ☐ AWARENESS ☐ EVALUATION ☐ CONVERSION

HOW WILL YOU TRACK SUCCESS? _____
_____

IS THE CALL TO ACTION CLEAR? ☐ YES ☐ NO   IS YOUR PIXEL INSTALLED? ☐ YES ☐ NO

AD BUDGET _____

AD DURATION _____ - _____

DETAILED AD CAMPAIGN TRACKER

AD HEADLINE 1

_____

AD HEADLINE 2

_____

AD TEXT

_____

_____

_____

_____

IMAGE IDEA

_____

_____

URL

_____

CALL TO ACTION

☐ SHOP NOW   ☐ DOWNLOAD   ☐ WATCH MORE   ☐ BOOK NOW

☐ LISTEN NOW   ☐ LEARN MORE   ☐ APPLY NOW   ☐ SIGN UP

☐ INSTALL NOW   ☐ DONATE NOW   ☐ USE APP   ☐ CONTACT US

AD TARGETS   AGE _____   LOCATION _____   GENDER _____

CUSTOM AUDIENCE _____   INTEREST _____

_____

WHAT IS THE GOAL FOR THE AD?   ☐ AWARENESS   ☐ EVALUATION   ☐ CONVERSION

HOW WILL YOU TRACK SUCCESS? _____

_____

IS THE CALL TO ACTION CLEAR? ☐ YES ☐ NO   IS YOUR PIXEL INSTALLED? ☐ YES ☐ NO

AD BUDGET _____

AD DURATION _____ - _____

DETAILED AD CAMPAIGN TRACKER

AD HEADLINE 1 _____

_____

AD HEADLINE 2 _____

_____

AD TEXT _____

_____

_____

_____

IMAGE IDEA _____

_____

URL _____

CALL TO ACTION
- ☐ SHOP NOW
- ☐ DOWNLOAD
- ☐ WATCH MORE
- ☐ BOOK NOW
- ☐ LISTEN NOW
- ☐ LEARN MORE
- ☐ APPLY NOW
- ☐ SIGN UP
- ☐ INSTALL NOW
- ☐ DONATE NOW
- ☐ USE APP
- ☐ CONTACT US

AD TARGETS AGE _____ LOCATION _____ GENDER _____

CUSTOM AUDIENCE _____ INTEREST _____

_____ _____

WHAT IS THE GOAL FOR THE AD? ☐ AWARENESS ☐ EVALUATION ☐ CONVERSION

HOW WILL YOU TRACK SUCCESS? _____

_____

IS THE CALL TO ACTION CLEAR? ☐ YES ☐ NO   IS YOUR PIXEL INSTALLED? ☐ YES ☐ NO

AD BUDGET _____

AD DURATION _____ - _____

ADVERTISING TRACKER

DESCRIPTION

FORMAT

START DATE

END DATE

CLICKS

SALES

NOTES

DESCRIPTION

FORMAT

START DATE

END DATE

CLICKS

SALES

NOTES

ADVERTISING TRACKER

DESCRIPTION

FORMAT

START DATE

END DATE

CLICKS

SALES

NOTES

DESCRIPTION

FORMAT

START DATE

END DATE

CLICKS

SALES

NOTES

MONTH OF _____

Monday	Tuesday	Wednesday	Thursday	Friday	Saturday	Sunday

Awareness Goals:

_____

_____

_____

_____

Evaluation Goals:

_____

_____

_____

_____

Conversion & Retention Goals:

_____

_____

_____

_____

WEEK OF _____

Monday	Tuesday	Wednesday	Thursday	Friday	Saturday	Sunday

Awareness Goals:

_____

_____

_____

Evaluation Goals:

_____

_____

_____

Conversion & Retention Goals:

_____

_____

_____

WEEK OF

Monday	Tuesday	Wednesday	Thursday	Friday	Saturday	Sunday

Awareness Goals:

Evaluation Goals:

Conversion & Retention Goals:

WEEK OF _____

Monday	Tuesday	Wednesday	Thursday	Friday	Saturday	Sunday

Awareness Goals:

Evaluation Goals:

Conversion & Retention Goals:

WEEK OF

Monday	Tuesday	Wednesday	Thursday	Friday	Saturday	Sunday

Awareness Goals:

Evaluation Goals:

Conversion & Retention Goals:

WEEK OF _____

Monday	Tuesday	Wednesday	Thursday	Friday	Saturday	Sunday

Awareness Goals:

_____
_____
_____
_____

Evaluation Goals:

_____
_____
_____
_____

Conversion & Retention Goals:

_____
_____
_____
_____

DETAILED AD CAMPAIGN TRACKER

AD HEADLINE 1 _____

_____

AD HEADLINE 2 _____

_____

AD TEXT _____

_____

_____

_____

IMAGE IDEA _____

_____

URL _____

CALL TO ACTION
☐ SHOP NOW ☐ DOWNLOAD ☐ WATCH MORE ☐ BOOK NOW
☐ LISTEN NOW ☐ LEARN MORE ☐ APPLY NOW ☐ SIGN UP
☐ INSTALL NOW ☐ DONATE NOW ☐ USE APP ☐ CONTACT US

AD TARGETS AGE _____ LOCATION _____ GENDER _____

CUSTOM AUDIENCE _____ INTEREST _____

_____ _____

WHAT IS THE GOAL FOR THE AD? ☐ AWARENESS ☐ EVALUATION ☐ CONVERSION

HOW WILL YOU TRACK SUCCESS? _____

_____

IS THE CALL TO ACTION CLEAR? ☐ YES ☐ NO   IS YOUR PIXEL INSTALLED? ☐ YES ☐ NO

AD BUDGET _____

AD DURATION _____

DETAILED AD CAMPAIGN TRACKER

AD HEADLINE 1
_____

_____

AD HEADLINE 2
_____

_____

AD TEXT
_____

_____

_____

_____

IMAGE IDEA
_____

_____

URL _____

CALL TO ACTION
☐ SHOP NOW ☐ DOWNLOAD ☐ WATCH MORE ☐ BOOK NOW

☐ LISTEN NOW ☐ LEARN MORE ☐ APPLY NOW ☐ SIGN UP

☐ INSTALL NOW ☐ DONATE NOW ☐ USE APP ☐ CONTACT US

AD TARGETS AGE _____ LOCATION _____ GENDER _____

CUSTOM AUDIENCE _____ INTEREST _____

_____ _____

WHAT IS THE GOAL FOR THE AD? ☐ AWARENESS ☐ EVALUATION ☐ CONVERSION

HOW WILL YOU TRACK SUCCESS? _____

_____

IS THE CALL TO ACTION CLEAR? ☐ YES ☐ NO   IS YOUR PIXEL INSTALLED? ☐ YES ☐ NO

AD BUDGET _____

AD DURATION _____ - _____

DETAILED AD CAMPAIGN TRACKER

AD HEADLINE 1 _____

_____

AD HEADLINE 2 _____

_____

AD TEXT _____

_____

_____

_____

IMAGE IDEA _____

_____

URL _____

CALL TO ACTION
- [ ] SHOP NOW
- [ ] DOWNLOAD
- [ ] WATCH MORE
- [ ] BOOK NOW
- [ ] LISTEN NOW
- [ ] LEARN MORE
- [ ] APPLY NOW
- [ ] SIGN UP
- [ ] INSTALL NOW
- [ ] DONATE NOW
- [ ] USE APP
- [ ] CONTACT US

AD TARGETS AGE _____ LOCATION _____ GENDER _____

CUSTOM AUDIENCE _____ INTEREST _____

_____ _____

WHAT IS THE GOAL FOR THE AD?
- [ ] AWARENESS
- [ ] EVALUATION
- [ ] CONVERSION

HOW WILL YOU TRACK SUCCESS? _____

_____

IS THE CALL TO ACTION CLEAR?
- [ ] YES
- [ ] NO

IS YOUR PIXEL INSTALLED?
- [ ] YES
- [ ] NO

AD BUDGET _____

AD DURATION _____ - _____

DETAILED AD CAMPAIGN TRACKER

AD HEADLINE 1 _____

_____

AD HEADLINE 2 _____

_____

AD TEXT _____

_____

_____

_____

IMAGE IDEA _____

_____

URL _____

CALL TO ACTION
- ☐ SHOP NOW
- ☐ DOWNLOAD
- ☐ WATCH MORE
- ☐ BOOK NOW
- ☐ LISTEN NOW
- ☐ LEARN MORE
- ☐ APPLY NOW
- ☐ SIGN UP
- ☐ INSTALL NOW
- ☐ DONATE NOW
- ☐ USE APP
- ☐ CONTACT US

AD TARGETS AGE _____ LOCATION _____ GENDER _____

CUSTOM AUDIENCE _____ INTEREST _____

_____ _____

WHAT IS THE GOAL FOR THE AD? ☐ AWARENESS ☐ EVALUATION ☐ CONVERSION

HOW WILL YOU TRACK SUCCESS? _____

_____

IS THE CALL TO ACTION CLEAR? ☐ YES ☐ NO   IS YOUR PIXEL INSTALLED? ☐ YES ☐ NO

AD BUDGET _____

AD DURATION _____

ADVERTISING TRACKER

DESCRIPTION

FORMAT

START DATE

END DATE

CLICKS

SALES

NOTES

DESCRIPTION

FORMAT

START DATE

END DATE

CLICKS

SALES

NOTES

ADVERTISING TRACKER

DESCRIPTION

FORMAT

START DATE

END DATE

CLICKS

SALES

NOTES

DESCRIPTION

FORMAT

START DATE

END DATE

CLICKS

SALES

NOTES

MONTH OF _____

Monday	Tuesday	Wednesday	Thursday	Friday	Saturday	Sunday

Awareness Goals:

_____

_____

_____

_____

Evaluation Goals:

_____

_____

_____

_____

Conversion & Retention Goals:

_____

_____

_____

_____

WEEK OF _____

Monday	Tuesday	Wednesday	Thursday	Friday	Saturday	Sunday

Awareness Goals:

_____
_____
_____
_____

Evaluation Goals:

_____
_____
_____
_____

Conversion & Retention Goals:

_____
_____
_____
_____

WEEK OF

Monday	Tuesday	Wednesday	Thursday	Friday	Saturday	Sunday

Awareness Goals:

Evaluation Goals:

Conversion & Retention Goals:

WEEK OF _____

Monday	Tuesday	Wednesday	Thursday	Friday	Saturday	Sunday

Awareness Goals:

_____
_____
_____
_____

Evaluation Goals:

_____
_____
_____
_____

Conversion & Retention Goals:

_____
_____
_____
_____

WEEK OF _____

Monday	Tuesday	Wednesday	Thursday	Friday	Saturday	Sunday

Awareness Goals:

_____
_____
_____
_____

Evaluation Goals:

_____
_____
_____
_____

Conversion & Retention Goals:

_____
_____
_____
_____

WEEK OF ___

Monday	Tuesday	Wednesday	Thursday	Friday	Saturday	Sunday

Awareness Goals:

_____
_____
_____
_____

Evaluation Goals:

_____
_____
_____
_____

Conversion & Retention Goals:

_____
_____
_____
_____

DETAILED AD CAMPAIGN TRACKER

AD HEADLINE 1

_____

_____

AD HEADLINE 2

_____

_____

AD TEXT

_____

_____

_____

_____

IMAGE IDEA

_____

_____

URL _____

CALL TO ACTION
☐ SHOP NOW ☐ DOWNLOAD ☐ WATCH MORE ☐ BOOK NOW

☐ LISTEN NOW ☐ LEARN MORE ☐ APPLY NOW ☐ SIGN UP

☐ INSTALL NOW ☐ DONATE NOW ☐ USE APP ☐ CONTACT US

AD TARGETS AGE _____ LOCATION _____ GENDER _____

CUSTOM AUDIENCE _____ INTEREST _____

_____

WHAT IS THE GOAL FOR THE AD? ☐ AWARENESS ☐ EVALUATION ☐ CONVERSION

HOW WILL YOU TRACK SUCCESS? _____

_____

IS THE CALL TO ACTION CLEAR? ☐ YES ☐ NO IS YOUR PIXEL INSTALLED? ☐ YES ☐ NO

AD BUDGET _____

AD DURATION _____ - _____

DETAILED AD CAMPAIGN TRACKER

AD HEADLINE 1 _____

_____

AD HEADLINE 2 _____

_____

AD TEXT _____

_____

_____

_____

IMAGE IDEA _____

_____

URL _____

CALL TO ACTION
- ☐ SHOP NOW
- ☐ DOWNLOAD
- ☐ WATCH MORE
- ☐ BOOK NOW
- ☐ LISTEN NOW
- ☐ LEARN MORE
- ☐ APPLY NOW
- ☐ SIGN UP
- ☐ INSTALL NOW
- ☐ DONATE NOW
- ☐ USE APP
- ☐ CONTACT US

AD TARGETS AGE _____ LOCATION _____ GENDER _____

CUSTOM AUDIENCE _____ INTEREST _____

_____ _____

WHAT IS THE GOAL FOR THE AD? ☐ AWARENESS ☐ EVALUATION ☐ CONVERSION

HOW WILL YOU TRACK SUCCESS? _____

_____

IS THE CALL TO ACTION CLEAR? ☐ YES ☐ NO   IS YOUR PIXEL INSTALLED? ☐ YES ☐ NO

AD BUDGET _____

AD DURATION _____ - _____

DETAILED AD CAMPAIGN TRACKER

AD HEADLINE 1 _____

_____

AD HEADLINE 2 _____

_____

AD TEXT _____

_____

_____

_____

IMAGE IDEA _____

_____

URL _____

CALL TO ACTION
- ☐ SHOP NOW
- ☐ DOWNLOAD
- ☐ WATCH MORE
- ☐ BOOK NOW
- ☐ LISTEN NOW
- ☐ LEARN MORE
- ☐ APPLY NOW
- ☐ SIGN UP
- ☐ INSTALL NOW
- ☐ DONATE NOW
- ☐ USE APP
- ☐ CONTACT US

AD TARGETS AGE _____ LOCATION _____ GENDER _____

CUSTOM AUDIENCE _____ INTEREST _____

_____ _____

WHAT IS THE GOAL FOR THE AD? ☐ AWARENESS ☐ EVALUATION ☐ CONVERSION

HOW WILL YOU TRACK SUCCESS? _____

_____

IS THE CALL TO ACTION CLEAR? ☐ YES ☐ NO   IS YOUR PIXEL INSTALLED? ☐ YES ☐ NO

AD BUDGET _____

AD DURATION _____ - _____

DETAILED AD CAMPAIGN TRACKER

AD HEADLINE 1
_____
_____

AD HEADLINE 2
_____
_____

AD TEXT
_____
_____
_____
_____

IMAGE IDEA
_____
_____

URL _____

CALL TO ACTION
☐ SHOP NOW ☐ DOWNLOAD ☐ WATCH MORE ☐ BOOK NOW
☐ LISTEN NOW ☐ LEARN MORE ☐ APPLY NOW ☐ SIGN UP
☐ INSTALL NOW ☐ DONATE NOW ☐ USE APP ☐ CONTACT US

AD TARGETS AGE _____ LOCATION _____ GENDER _____

CUSTOM AUDIENCE _____ INTEREST _____
_____ _____

WHAT IS THE GOAL FOR THE AD? ☐ AWARENESS ☐ EVALUATION ☐ CONVERSION

HOW WILL YOU TRACK SUCCESS? _____
_____

IS THE CALL TO ACTION CLEAR? ☐ YES ☐ NO   IS YOUR PIXEL INSTALLED? ☐ YES ☐ NO

AD BUDGET _____

AD DURATION _____ - _____

ADVERTISING TRACKER

DESCRIPTION

FORMAT

START DATE

END DATE

CLICKS

SALES

NOTES

DESCRIPTION

FORMAT

START DATE

END DATE

CLICKS

SALES

NOTES

ADVERTISING TRACKER

DESCRIPTION

FORMAT

START DATE

END DATE

CLICKS

SALES

NOTES

DESCRIPTION

FORMAT

START DATE

END DATE

CLICKS

SALES

NOTES

MONTH OF _____

Monday	Tuesday	Wednesday	Thursday	Friday	Saturday	Sunday

Awareness Goals:

_____

_____

_____

_____

_____

Evaluation Goals:

_____

_____

_____

_____

_____

Conversion & Retention Goals:

_____

_____

_____

_____

_____

WEEK OF

Monday	Tuesday	Wednesday	Thursday	Friday	Saturday	Sunday

Awareness Goals:

Evaluation Goals:

Conversion & Retention Goals:

WEEK OF

Monday	Tuesday	Wednesday	Thursday	Friday	Saturday	Sunday

Awareness Goals:

Evaluation Goals:

Conversion & Retention Goals:

WEEK OF _____

Monday	Tuesday	Wednesday	Thursday	Friday	Saturday	Sunday

Awareness Goals:

_____
_____
_____
_____

Evaluation Goals:

_____
_____
_____
_____

Conversion & Retention Goals:

_____
_____
_____
_____

WEEK OF

Monday	Tuesday	Wednesday	Thursday	Friday	Saturday	Sunday

Awareness Goals:

_____

_____

_____

_____

Evaluation Goals:

_____

_____

_____

_____

Conversion & Retention Goals:

_____

_____

_____

_____

WEEK OF _____

Monday	Tuesday	Wednesday	Thursday	Friday	Saturday	Sunday

Awareness Goals:

_____

_____

_____

Evaluation Goals:

_____

_____

_____

Conversion & Retention Goals:

_____

_____

_____

DETAILED AD CAMPAIGN TRACKER

AD HEADLINE 1 _____

_____

AD HEADLINE 2 _____

_____

AD TEXT _____

_____

_____

_____

IMAGE IDEA _____

_____

URL _____

CALL TO ACTION
- ☐ SHOP NOW ☐ DOWNLOAD ☐ WATCH MORE ☐ BOOK NOW
- ☐ LISTEN NOW ☐ LEARN MORE ☐ APPLY NOW ☐ SIGN UP
- ☐ INSTALL NOW ☐ DONATE NOW ☐ USE APP ☐ CONTACT US

AD TARGETS AGE _____ LOCATION _____ GENDER _____

CUSTOM AUDIENCE _____ INTEREST _____

_____ _____

WHAT IS THE GOAL FOR THE AD? ☐ AWARENESS ☐ EVALUATION ☐ CONVERSION

HOW WILL YOU TRACK SUCCESS? _____

_____

IS THE CALL TO ACTION CLEAR? ☐ YES ☐ NO   IS YOUR PIXEL INSTALLED? ☐ YES ☐ NO

AD BUDGET _____

AD DURATION _____ - _____

DETAILED AD CAMPAIGN TRACKER

AD HEADLINE 1

_____

_____

AD HEADLINE 2

_____

_____

AD TEXT

_____

_____

_____

_____

IMAGE IDEA

_____

_____

URL

_____

CALL TO ACTION
☐ SHOP NOW ☐ DOWNLOAD ☐ WATCH MORE ☐ BOOK NOW
☐ LISTEN NOW ☐ LEARN MORE ☐ APPLY NOW ☐ SIGN UP
☐ INSTALL NOW ☐ DONATE NOW ☐ USE APP ☐ CONTACT US

AD TARGETS AGE _____ LOCATION _____ GENDER _____

CUSTOM AUDIENCE _____ INTEREST _____

_____   _____

WHAT IS THE GOAL FOR THE AD? ☐ AWARENESS ☐ EVALUATION ☐ CONVERSION

HOW WILL YOU TRACK SUCCESS? _____

_____

IS THE CALL TO ACTION CLEAR? ☐ YES ☐ NO   IS YOUR PIXEL INSTALLED? ☐ YES ☐ NO

AD BUDGET _____

AD DURATION _____ - _____

DETAILED AD CAMPAIGN TRACKER

AD HEADLINE 1 _____

_____

AD HEADLINE 2 _____

_____

AD TEXT _____

_____

_____

_____

IMAGE IDEA _____

_____

URL _____

CALL TO ACTION
☐ SHOP NOW ☐ DOWNLOAD ☐ WATCH MORE ☐ BOOK NOW

☐ LISTEN NOW ☐ LEARN MORE ☐ APPLY NOW ☐ SIGN UP

☐ INSTALL NOW ☐ DONATE NOW ☐ USE APP ☐ CONTACT US

AD TARGETS AGE _____ LOCATION _____ GENDER _____

CUSTOM AUDIENCE _____ INTEREST _____

_____

WHAT IS THE GOAL FOR THE AD? ☐ AWARENESS ☐ EVALUATION ☐ CONVERSION

HOW WILL YOU TRACK SUCCESS? _____

_____

IS THE CALL TO ACTION CLEAR? ☐ YES ☐ NO   IS YOUR PIXEL INSTALLED? ☐ YES ☐ NO

AD BUDGET _____

AD DURATION _____ - _____

DETAILED AD CAMPAIGN TRACKER

AD HEADLINE 1

_____

_____

AD HEADLINE 2

_____

_____

AD TEXT

_____

_____

_____

_____

IMAGE IDEA

_____

_____

URL

CALL TO ACTION
☐ SHOP NOW   ☐ DOWNLOAD   ☐ WATCH MORE   ☐ BOOK NOW
☐ LISTEN NOW   ☐ LEARN MORE   ☐ APPLY NOW   ☐ SIGN UP
☐ INSTALL NOW   ☐ DONATE NOW   ☐ USE APP   ☐ CONTACT US

AD TARGETS   AGE _____   LOCATION _____   GENDER _____

CUSTOM AUDIENCE _____   INTEREST _____

_____   _____

WHAT IS THE GOAL FOR THE AD?   ☐ AWARENESS   ☐ EVALUATION   ☐ CONVERSION

HOW WILL YOU TRACK SUCCESS? _____

_____

IS THE CALL TO ACTION CLEAR?   ☐ YES   ☐ NO   IS YOUR PIXEL INSTALLED?   ☐ YES   ☐ NO

AD BUDGET _____

AD DURATION _____ - _____

ADVERTISING TRACKER

DESCRIPTION

FORMAT

START DATE

END DATE

CLICKS

SALES

NOTES

DESCRIPTION

FORMAT

START DATE

END DATE

CLICKS

SALES

NOTES

ADVERTISING TRACKER

DESCRIPTION

FORMAT

START DATE

END DATE

CLICKS

SALES

NOTES

DESCRIPTION

FORMAT

START DATE

END DATE

CLICKS

SALES

NOTES

NOTES

NOTES

NOTES

NOTES

NOTES

NOTES

NOTES

NOTES

NOTES

NOTES

NOTES

NOTES

NOTES

NOTES

NOTES

NOTES

NOTES

NOTES

NOTES

NOTES

NOTES

NOTES

NOTES

NOTES

NOTES

NOTES

NOTES

NOTES

NOTES

NOTES

Made in the
USA
Monee, IL